OVERCOMING ADDICTION™

METHAMPHETAMINE AND STIMULANT ABUSE

BETHANY BRYAN

Rosen
YA
New York

Published in 2019 by The Rosen Publishing Group, Inc.
29 East 21st Street, New York, NY 10010

Library of Congress Cataloging-in-Publication Data

Names: Bryan, Bethany, author.
Title: Methamphetamine and stimulant abuse / Bethany Bryan.
Description: New York : Rosen Publishing, 2019. | Series: Overcoming addiction | Audience: Grades 7–12. | Includes bibliographical references and index.
Identifiers: LCCN 2017044962| ISBN 9781508179405 (library bound) | ISBN 9781508179573 (pbk.)
Subjects: LCSH: Amphetamine abuse—Juvenile literature. | Ice (Drug)—Juvenile literature. | Stimulants—Juvenile literature.
Classification: LCC RC568.A45 B79 2017 | DDC 613.8/4—dc23
LC record available at https://lccn.loc.gov/2017044962

Manufactured in the United States of America

CONTENTS

INTRODUCTION

Janelle Hornickel and her boyfriend, Michael Wamsley, were about twenty-three miles (thirty-seven kilometers) from their apartment in Omaha, Nebraska, when they got lost in a snowstorm. It was late at night, the roads were icy, and the truck they were driving spun off the road and into a gravel pit. The pair did what many would do in their situation: they called 911. But when the dispatcher asked for their location, Hornickel could only provide the "trees above the Mandalay." The Mandalay was the name of the apartment complex where the couple lived, in Omaha. Police went to the Mandalay to investigate but found nothing.

Wamsley called 911 again around 1:05 a.m. to say that the couple had left the truck and were trying to find their apartment. But they were still miles from home. In 2005, Nebraska didn't have an accurate GPS system for tracking cell phones. Police dispatch could tell that the cell signal was coming from nearby Sarpy County, but there was no way to pinpoint an exact location for the truck and its occupants. All the police could do was drive to possible locations near where the cell signal had originated and hope they would chance upon the couple. But they didn't

Crystal meth, shown here in the custody of the Drug Enforcement Agency (DEA), is an inorganic, highly addictive substance that can cause permanent damage to the body.

have much time. In subzero temperatures, if Wamsley and Hornickel had left the truck, they were in serious danger.

The last call to 911 came in around 4:20 a.m. Michael Wamsley said simply, "I have just escaped. Please come get me." His body was found the next morning. Hornickel's was found six days later. The couple had frozen to death in the snowstorm. Neither was wearing a winter coat.

Toxicology tests were run on both Wamsley and Hornickel, and both were found to have significant amounts of methamphetamine in their systems at the time of their deaths. A small amount of crystal meth was found in the truck. Crystal meth, a crystallized form of methamphetamine, has been known to cause hallucinations and a rise in body temperature, which would explain the couple's disorientation and the lack of coats. Being in a snowstorm on a freezing cold night is dangerous enough on its own, but the addition of being high on crystal meth proved deadly for Michael Wamsley and Janelle Hornickel.

Crystal meth is part of a group of drugs known as stimulants. Stimulants increase the user's heart rate and can make the user feel more energetic, even euphoric. That is why doctors sometimes prescribe certain types of stimulants to treat ailments like narcolepsy, depression, and attention deficit hyperactivity disorder (ADHD). However, the body can come to crave and eventually require these types of drugs in order to function. This is addiction. People can become addicted to stimulants, taking more and more until they are consuming dangerous amounts of the drug.

Illicit stimulant drugs, such as crystal meth and cocaine, can offer a similar but significantly more dangerous high and are not regulated by the Food and Drug Administration (FDA) the way that prescription drugs are. Therefore, users have no way of knowing if the drugs they are using are pure or even the substance they were promised.

Due to tragedies like the deaths of Michael Wamsley and Janelle Hornickel, it's important to be aware of stimulant drugs and the effects they have on the body in the short and long term. Being aware of the signs of addiction and the tools you need to help yourself or someone you love recover can help prevent further tragedies due to stimulant abuse.

CHAPTER 1

WHAT ARE STIMULANTS?

Stimulant drugs are everywhere. Chances are very good you've ingested a stimulant within your lifetime, and you might not have even known it. Caffeine, found in sodas, coffee, tea, and even chocolate, is a stimulant. Nicotine is also a stimulant, so even if you don't smoke but you've passed a smoker on the street and inhaled smoke secondhand, you've been affected by this type of drug. If you suffer from certain illnesses, you might even take a type of stimulant prescribed by your doctor. But what

Even legal drugs, like caffeine, nicotine, and alcohol, can have negative effects on the body. All drugs change how the brain responds to normal stimuli.

are stimulants? What do they do? And why do people become addicted to them? Let's begin by looking at some of the different types of this class of drug.

A FIELD GUIDE TO COMMON STIMULANTS

There are three basic types of stimulant drugs: ones you can obtain with a doctor's prescription; illicit, or illegal, stimulant drugs; and caffeine and nicotine, which can be found in food, beverages, cigarettes, and other products that contain tobacco. Stimulants are any type of drug that causes the brain to release a higher than normal amount of the neurotransmitter dopamine. (We'll talk more about this in the next section.) You can become addicted to all types of stimulants. In fact, some people might suffer from stimulant addiction without even realizing it.

CAFFEINE AND NICOTINE

Caffeine and nicotine are the two of the most widely available types of stimulants. In the United States, individuals over the age of eighteen can legally purchase tobacco products. However, caffeine products can be purchased at any age.

According to a 2013 survey in *USA Today,* Americans drink around 587 million cups of coffee daily, making many of them dependent on the stimulant caffeine.

Nicotine is actually found in a variety of plant sources, including eggplant, cauliflower, and potatoes—but these contain only a trace amount of nicotine. (Don't worry, if you really like eggplant Parmesan, it's probably not because of a nicotine addiction.) The main source of nicotine, however, is tobacco. Tobacco is a large, leafy plant that has been grown by farmers for centuries in order to make products like cigarettes, cigars, and chewing tobacco. The leaves of the tobacco plant contain nicotine, which is a natural insecticide that protects the plant. In other words, nicotine is a type of poison, although according to the US National Library of Medicine and National Institutes of Health, a person would have to ingest around sixty milligrams of nicotine for the dose to be fatal. A smoker absorbs only about one milligram of nicotine while smoking a cigarette.

Many people believe that it's healthier to use smokeless products like e-cigarettes, which turn the nicotine into vapor, rather than smoke. But if you use an e-cigarette, you are still ingesting nicotine. Patches and gum that are designed to help smokers quit also contain nicotine.

Like tobacco, caffeine also occurs naturally in plants—in this case most commonly tea, coffee, and cacao plants. The caffeine in these types of plants helps to ward off insects, as well as changing the chemicals in the soil around the plant to help protect the plant from types of vegetation that might harm it. By the time people consume caffeine, it is in the form of coffee, teas, soft drinks, energy drinks, and chocolate.

Caffeine is the most frequently used stimulant in the world and consumption is legal in every country. But while caffeine addiction is common, death from a caffeine overdose is rare. An average adult can safely consume around four hundred milligrams of caffeine a day, according to the Mayo Clinic.

To overdose on coffee, you would have to consume between five and ten grams—the amount found in a minimum of twelve and a half Venti-sized regular brew Starbucks coffees.

A DOCTOR'S PRESCRIPTION

There are three types of stimulants that can be prescribed by doctors for the treatment of ADHD, narcolepsy, and depression:

- amphetamines (sold as Adderall or Dexadrine)
- methylphenidate (sold as Ritalin or Concerta)
- methamphetamine hydrochloride (sold as Desoxyn)

All of these drugs are addictive if not used precisely as a doctor instructs. Methamphetamine hydrochloride is a controversial drug because it is made up of the same compounds as crystal meth and is therefore administered very carefully. To acquire or use these drugs without a prescription is illegal. Doctors start a patient on a low dose of the drug and gradually increase it, as necessary, until they achieve the desired effect and the patient feels better and their symptoms are under control. Doctors keep a close eye on patients to make sure that they are only taking the prescribed dose. If a patient has a past issue with drug addiction, doctors may find another type of treatment.

So what's the difference between simply using the drug and abusing it? There are a few ways that people abuse prescription stimulants.

- They take a medication that was prescribed to someone else. This can include taking medications out of someone else's medicine cabinet.

- They take medication in a manner other than the way it was prescribed. For example, crushing a drug and snorting it, rather than ingesting it via the mouth in capsule form. This changes the way that the body absorbs the drug and can be very harmful.
- They take the drug with the purpose of achieving a high.
- They combine the drug with other drugs to achieve a different, more intense effect. Doctors advise not consuming alcohol while taking certain prescriptions because these effects can be dangerous.

A HISTORY OF METH

When amphetamine was first synthesized in Germany in 1887 by a Romanian chemist named Lazar Edelenu, no one knew quite what to do with it. The drug didn't seem to have a practical medical use at the time, so it sat on the shelf until the 1920s when doctors began experimenting with using it to treat asthma, allergies, and colds. It was around that time that doctors began to notice that it also acted as a stimulant. Methamphetamine, a more potent version of the same drug, was synthesized in the form of a soluble crystal in 1919 in Japan. Its effects as a stimulant were more powerful and longer lasting, which made it seem like a more useful drug. During World War II, both sides gave their pilots methamphetamine to help them stay awake and alert.

Later, truck drivers began to use methamphetamine to help them stay awake during long hauls that required them to travel late at night. Athletes and students soon began to take these drugs as well, which helped them

(continued on the next page)

(continued from the previous page)

perform better or stay up later to study. Others simply enjoyed the hallucinogenic effects or feeling of elation meth provided. Cases of methamphetamine abuse grew in number, as did concern that it was not a safe, harmless product after all. Finally, in 1970, methamphetamine was declared illegal by the US government.

During World War II, pilots on both sides were often given stimulants like methamphetamine to keep them awake and alert for battle.

ILLEGAL STIMULANTS

Illegal stimulants include drugs like crystal meth, cocaine, and MDMA (more commonly known as ecstasy) since all three have similar effects on the body. Here, however, we will focus on crystal meth, a form of methamphetamine that is combined in such a way that it forms crystals, which are then smoked, crushed and snorted, or dissolved in water and injected. This drug is also known as ice, speed, glass, or crank, among other common street names.

Methamphetamine often comes in the form of "crystals" that are crushed and then snorted, injected, or smoked. All methods of ingestion are dangerous.

Crystal meth is made of a dangerous combination of chemicals, including acetone, which is found in paint thinner and nail polish remover; anhydrous ammonia, found in fertilizer; lye; sulfuric acid; and others. The main stimulant element of methamphetamine often comes from pseudoephedrine, found in certain allergy and cold medications. This is why it has become more difficult to purchase cold medication, because illegal drug manufacturers buy the pills to produce crystal meth.

Crystal meth is highly addictive and the long-term effects can include brain damage, memory loss, weight loss, damage to teeth, violent behavior, mood changes, hallucinations, and even death. Between 2012 and 2013, DrugAbuse.com reported that there were 133,000 new users of methamphetamine. The average age of a meth user is 19.7 years. While the number of meth users has been steadily decreasing since the early 2000s, meth use is still a problem largely because it can be made using readily available chemicals and can be purchased for less than other types of drugs. This helps it spread through lower income and rural areas.

Additionally, many of the ingredients of methamphetamine are flammable, corrosive, and dangerous on their own, even before they're combined. People who make methamphetamine, often called cooks, are exposed to these chemicals on a daily basis, risking injury, arrest, and even death.

MYTHS AND FACTS

MYTH: If a doctor prescribed it, the drug is totally safe for anyone to take.

FACT: There is a reason that doctors write prescriptions and you can't just run to the pharmacy and pick up Adderall without one. Drugs can be harmful if a doctor isn't monitoring the effect that the drug is having on your body. If a doctor writes you a prescription, he or she has considered the amount of drug that you will need for your height and weight and can tell you how many times daily you will need to take it to achieve the desired effects of the drug. Your doctor can also check back with you to make sure that the drug is having a positive effect and not a negative one. Passing a dose of Adderall to a friend might seem harmless. But not only is it illegal, the dosage might be too high or cause unwanted side effects.

MYTH: Stimulants can help make me a better student.

FACT: While it's true that stimulants can help increase focus for a short period of time, they can also decrease appetite, make you more irritable, and cause heart issues and high blood pressure, in addition to a variety of other negative effects. And if you get into the habit of taking stimulants every time you have to take a test, it will become harder and harder to tell when you actually need help focusing and when you just need to use the drug.

(CONTINUED ON THE NEXT PAGE)

(CONTINUED FROM THE PREVIOUS PAGE)

MYTH: Myth: It's impossible to quit using meth.

FACT: While it is true that the recovery rate for meth addicts is low and many relapse to using again, recovery is not impossible with the right tools and support from friends and family.

MYTH: It takes one try to become addicted to crystal meth

FACT: While crystal meth is a dangerous drug, it takes more than one use to become addicted. Some studies have shown that it takes between two and five years of use for most meth users to become psychologically and physically addicted to the drug.

CHAPTER 2

STIMULANTS AND THE BODY

Every type of stimulant has one thing in common. When ingested, stimulants make the body release the neurotransmitter dopamine. Dopamine is a chemical that sends a signal to the brain that something is pleasurable. Basically, dopamine makes you feel happy, if just temporarily. If you score a touchdown and win the football game for your team, your body is releasing dopamine. Athletes often say that winning gives them a high. It's true! They're experiencing the rush of dopamine. If your crush talks to you at school, the euphoria you feel afterward is also due to dopamine. This chemical is what gives you that excited, squishy feeling at the beginning of a relationship.

DOPAMINE AND THE REWARD CIRCUIT

The part of the brain in charge of pleasure and happiness is often called the reward circuit. This includes the amygdala, the hippocampus, and the prefrontal cortex. The neurons that

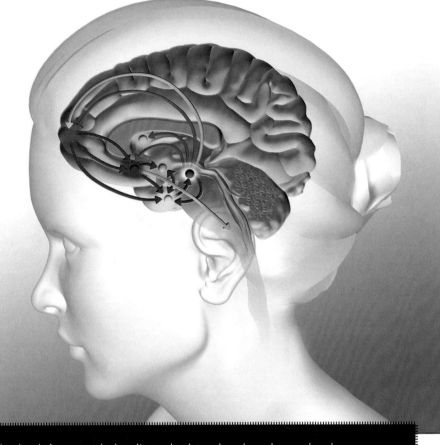

The brain's reward circuit works by releasing dopamine in response to something positive. Stimulants work by tricking the brain into releasing dopamine.

make up the brain release neurotransmitters, like dopamine, in response to a signal sent through the nervous system.

For instance, it's your birthday and you take your first bite of chocolate cake. You feel happy because your nervous system has sent a signal to your brain that this is a happy moment and it's time to release dopamine. As dopamine spreads across the neurons, it activates them by binding to the receiving neuron receptors. Dopamine has a special receptor that it bonds to on a neuron, kind of like a lock and key. The result is a feeling of happiness.

Stimulant drugs increase the amount of dopamine released by the neurons. A person trying crystal meth for the first time might feel joy or heightened energy. These feelings aren't due to a positive stimulus but are simply the chemical effects of the drug on the body. So when a person comes down from the drug, the user might crave the effects of it again as a method of coping with depression, anxiety, or a negative life situation. As a person takes more of the drug, the body starts to need more and more of it in order to achieve the same effect. This need is addiction.

THE SHORT-TERM EFFECTS OF STIMULANT USE

If you've ever drunk a cup of coffee, tea, or an energy drink before a big test, you know the small-scale effects a stimulant can have on the body. You might feel yourself becoming a little bit more aware and more awake. You may even feel happy or excited about the test's outcome. If you don't ingest caffeinated beverages frequently, you may feel a little bit jittery or anxious. When you ingest an amphetamine-based stimulant or illegal stimulant, the effects are virtually the same, just on a larger scale.

There can be positive effects when people use certain stimulants. A person with depression who takes a dose of a prescription stimulant may experience a feeling of happiness. A patient who suffers from narcolepsy may discover that with the use of prescription meds, he or she might be able to stay awake during class or at work. Stimulants, when used correctly, can be life changing for those suffering from certain disorders. Positive effects can include excitement, increased energy, heightened focus, and

People who suffer from certain illnesses, like depression, can actually be helped by stimulants. But overuse and abuse can have the opposite effect.

even euphoria. However, every drug has side effects, and when a prescription drug is abused, the side effects slowly start to outweigh the positive effects the drug might be having on the body.

Abuse of prescription stimulants can lead to effects like frequent headaches, nausea, mood swings, extreme anxiety, dizziness, increased heart rate, and high blood pressure, among others.

Prescription drugs are designed for a slow release into the body when ingested. The above effects occur over a longer period of time. When a person uses a more powerful, more dangerous stimulant like methamphetamine, the drug takes effect more quickly and the high is more intense. But the effects also fade quickly. This is why people who abuse drugs like crystal meth tend to binge on the drug, rewarding themselves with a high again and again. In the short term, people who abuse any type of methamphetamine may also experience insomnia, anxiety, and mood swings, among the other side effects. But the binges and increased use make the user dependent on the drug more quickly, which can lead to more serious long-term effects and addiction.

DRUGS AND YOUR HEALTH

In addition to the risk of overdose and the basic effects of the drug on the body, drug use can also put you at risk for a number of other medical issues.

- Risk of disease: Drug use and diseases like HIV and hepatitis often go hand in hand. Lowered inhibition because of a drug can lead to unsafe sexual activity and sharing of needles, which can spread disease. Drug use also weakens the immune system, leaving the body less able to fight an infection.
- Damage to the heart: Drug use can weaken the walls of the heart, causing problems even after a user kicks the habit. This damage can

(continued on the next page)

(continued from the previous page)

lead to heart attacks or strokes. You can also risk bacterial infection in the veins and heart valves if the equipment you are using to inject a drug is not clean.

- In addition to damage to the brain and nervous system, those who abuse methamphetamine might also experience long-term mental health issues, including mood disorders, anxiety, and impulse control.

THE LONG-TERM EFFECTS OF STIMULANT USE

Over time, as the body continues to ingest stimulants again and again, it begins to require more of the drug in order to obtain the wanted effect. This is often called building a tolerance. As a person begins to increase the amount of the drug he or she is taking, the effects on the body also change. Long-term abuse of prescription stimulants can lead to hallucinations, paranoia, extreme cravings for the drug, respiratory issues, and even violent behavior. Long-term effects of methamphetamine use can also include severe dental issues (sometimes called meth mouth), extreme weight loss, and psychosis—often resembling schizophrenia. The changes to a user's body begin to become apparent to friends and family. Meth use may begin to make a person look much older than he or she is. Many meth addicts begin to obsessively pick at their skin, leaving open sores on the face. Some addicts experience the sensation of insects crawling on their bodies. Addicts tend to stop taking care of their bodies, resulting in starvation and dehydration, which only makes the physical effects of the drug on the body worse.

Taking care of your teeth and visiting the dentist regularly are a must for everyone. Long-term meth users often suffer from gum disease and even tooth loss.

Long-term effects also include social issues. Addicts often experience financial difficulties, leading to homelessness and crime as they spend more and more money to buy the drug and resort to extremes in order to obtain money. Addicts may lose their jobs or face arrest, prosecution, and jail time. Addiction also takes a toll on personal relationships. Friends and family members may begin to distance themselves from an addict, leading to isolation and increased depression. And when an addict is face to face with the negative effects of a drug habit, he or she may resort to simply using more of the drug in order to cope.

OVERDOSE: WHAT IT LOOKS LIKE AND WHAT TO DO

A drug overdose can happen in a few different ways. An acute overdose occurs when an individual takes a large amount of a drug all at once. This often happens to first-time drug users who are not able to recognize the normal effects of the drug on the body or don't know when they've had too much. Acute overdose can also occur if someone ingests a drug thinking it's one kind

EMERGENCY DEPARTMENT
Departamento de Emergencias

01601

Don't take any chances if you think someone might be suffering an overdose. Call 911 right away and stay with the person until paramedics arrive.

of drug when it's really another. Chronic overdose describes the effects of long-term abuse of a drug. The risk of an overdose increases if a user combines the drug with another type of drug or with alcohol, injects the drug directly into the bloodstream, or has a heart condition or other type of disease.

Some signs of a stimulant overdose include enlarged pupils, difficulty breathing, chest pain, hallucinations, high body temperature, nausea, agitation, and even seizures or unconsciousness.

An overdose is extremely dangerous. If you notice any of the above symptoms, call 911 immediately. You'll want to take note of a few specific things in order to help. The 911 dispatcher will ask for the age of the victim, the type of drug he or she was using, how it was ingested, and how recently the drug was taken. Although you may be afraid of getting a friend or family member—or even yourself—in trouble, it's important to be as honest as possible. If the individual is unconscious, monitor his or her breathing. If the victim begins to vomit, roll the person onto his or her side to prevent choking. And never put fingers or other objects in a person's mouth during a seizure. Stay with the person until help arrives and be prepared to answer questions. How you react in the case of a drug overdose is often a matter of life and death.

CHAPTER 3

THE DISEASE OF ADDICTION

You'll often hear addicts and drug therapists referring to addiction as a disease. This is actually a pretty modern concept. For years, people assumed that anyone who did drugs lacked morals, had no self-discipline, and were selfish. Drug use was seen more as a character flaw than a health problem, and the solution was often prayer or a stay in a mental institution. In 1935, Dr. Bob Smith and Bill Wilson founded a rehabilitation program called Alcoholics Anonymous (AA), through which alcoholics could find support with other people who understood their problem. More drug-specific programs—Narcotics Anonymous, Cocaine Anonymous, and Marijuana Anonymous—later branched off from AA. These groups allowed for a more empathetic approach to addiction.

The idea of addiction being a disease has become fairly well established in the medical community today. Many doctors are trying to change the way that people view addiction, in order to help addicts get the care they need.

Members of Narcotics Anonymous often receive small tags or chips to celebrate sobriety milestones. These small tokens are often invaluable to their recipients.

We're still learning about what causes addiction, why some people can make a decision to quit and follow through while others can't, and the best treatment strategies for future care. Whether addiction is actually a disease or something doctors have yet to uncover, the reality of addiction remains. But the most important thing to understand, when it comes to addiction, is that it is not a character flaw or a sign of weakness—it's a condition of the human body and should be treated with care.

ARE YOU OR A LOVED ONE AN ADDICT?

When we see drug addiction portrayed in movies and television, it's often with the addict looking sick or thin or shaking from withdrawal. The addict might be committing a crime or being victimized by someone else. Outwardly, according to movies and TV, you can easily recognize an addict. But addiction is rarely that simple. Anyone can be an addict, and addicts often look like anybody else.

THE SIGNS OF ADDICTION

There are many ways to recognize addiction in yourself and others. If you are concerned that you might be an addict, consider the following:

- Do you get the urge to use the drug regularly?
- Do you plan ahead so that you won't run out of the drug?
- Do you find ways to buy the drug even though you don't have the financial means to do so?
- Do you find yourself avoiding spending time with friends and family or forgetting events that would have been important to you previously?
- Do you experience withdrawal symptoms—fatigue, itching, paranoia, suicidal thoughts, or other feelings of unease—while not taking the drug?

The previous are all signs that you might be experiencing addiction. If you suspect that someone you know might be facing an issue with addiction to prescription or illegal stimulants, keep an eye out for bursts of energy followed by signs of fatigue; mood swings; weight loss; dilated pupils; frequent scratching or picking at the skin, open sores on the face, or acne; secretive behavior; stomach pain or headaches; or disinterest in social events or people.

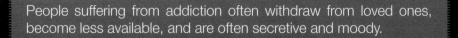

People suffering from addiction often withdraw from loved ones, become less available, and are often secretive and moody.

THE ROOTS OF ADDICTION

What causes addiction? There are five main factors that can lead to substance abuse and addiction. Some people might be affected by one or more of these factors.

A HIGH-STRESS LIFESTYLE

People often abuse drugs because they're trying to cope with something stressful or difficult in their lives. For example, financial analysts working on Wall Street tend to work long hours and face stressful situations as the stock market goes up and down. In order to work long hours, many people in high-stress situations turn to stimulants, often Adderall or other amphetamines.

SEVERE PHYSICAL OR MENTAL TRAUMA

Some addicts have experienced a trauma or injury that led them to drug abuse. According to statistics from the National Center for Post-Traumatic Stress Disorder (PTSD), two out of ten veterans with PTSD also struggle with substance abuse. Prescription meds that help ease the pain of a physical injury are often used carefully at first. But after some period of time, many people find that they can no longer function without the drug.

MENTAL HEALTH CONDITIONS

Actress Carrie Fisher, famous for playing Princess Leia in the original *Star Wars* trilogy, spoke very candidly about her struggles with both drug addiction and bipolar disorder, a mental illness

Actress Carrie Fisher often turned to drug use during her life to help cope with bipolar disorder. This is a common cause of addiction.

characterized by periods of elation and activity, followed by depressive episodes. To cope with the illness, Fisher turned to drugs at an early age. In a *Los Angeles Times* article written shortly after Fisher's death in 2016, Adam Leventhal, the director of the University of Southern California's Health, Emotion, and Addiction Laboratory, said that people with mental illness often use drugs to cope since drugs, "'trick the human brain into believing'" they're needed to feel right." Carrie Fisher was quoted as saying "drugs made me feel more normal" in a 2001 interview with *Psychology Today*.

GENETICS

Many in the scientific community believe that one of the biggest risk factors for drug abuse is in your genes. Some experts believe that a single gene or a gene mutation might be responsible for a person's predisposition to addiction. Doctors are still trying to learn all they can and hope that one day a simple genetics test will help patients understand and even prevent struggles with addiction.

EXPOSURE TO DRUGS AT A YOUNG AGE

Children and teens tend to have a lower level of impulse control than adults. They may not yet understand the consequences of drug abuse. So when children and teens are exposed to drugs at an early age, they tend to be more likely to experiment with them. Actor Robert Downey Jr., who has played Iron Man in multiple films, said in a 2014 interview with ABC that his father, Robert Downey, was the one who introduced him to drugs as a child. Robert Downey Jr. struggled with addiction throughout his twenties, finally kicking the habit for good in 2003.

Robert Downey Jr., famous for his role as Iron Man in the *Avengers* films, struggled with drug addiction starting early in his life.

COMING TO TERMS WITH YOUR ADDICTION

Coming to terms with an addiction can be a difficult experience. Perhaps friends or family have confronted you about the issue. Or maybe you came to the conclusion that you struggle with addiction all on your own. Realizing you have a problem is a big step. You might not be ready to immediately turn things around, and that's okay. Start by opening up to a friend, family member, or someone else you feel you can trust.

Schedule an appointment with a physician. Patients are protected by privacy laws, so your doctor cannot legally share any information with your parents without your permission—the only exception to this rule is if you are in immediate danger of harming yourself. (They also can't report you to law enforcement.) It's important to be honest with your doctor, even if you're embarrassed or ashamed. A doctor's job is to help you, and asking for help is an important first step.

If you don't have access to health care and don't feel safe reaching out to someone you know, you may want to call a drug abuse hotline. Calls are anonymous, and trained drug counselors are experienced in offering the best advice for your situation. You can also reach out to drug counselors in your area by checking their credentials online through services like the *Psychology Today* website. Many drug counselors offer low-cost therapy or can recommend a counselor who can work with your budget or provide guidance for free. Counselors are also barred from sharing personal information about you with others, unless, again, you are in danger of harming yourself.

One of the biggest hurdles you now face is figuring out what comes next for you, and the first step is to begin building your support base, whether it consists of friends, family, or just a voice over the phone.

COPING WITH SOMEONE ELSE'S ADDICTION

Learning that someone you love is suffering from addiction can fill you with a multitude of emotions, and sometimes that can be confusing. You might feel embarrassed or angry; you might feel sad or betrayed. You might even feel numb or deny to yourself that this is happening. You might feel all of these things at different times. These are all perfectly normal feelings. Everyone copes differently. It's important during these early stages to reach out to those around you for support. A friend, parent, grandparent, or other trusted individual is a good place to start. Seeing a therapist who specializes in drug addiction and treatment might also be a good option, if it is financially feasible for you and your family. There are also support groups for those who are coping with a loved one's addiction, such as Al-Anon, which are free to attend. Smaller groups within your community might also be available. If you're curious about where to go for support, look online for groups in your area. Remember that you do not have to cope all on your own.

CHAPTER 4

DRUGS AND CR1ME

Drugs have been a part of American culture since the 1800s, with the arrival of substances like opium and cocaine in the United States. At the time, these drugs were prized for their medicinal uses. Opium was often (and continues to be to this day) used for pain relief. Cocaine was sold as a numbing agent for surgeries and was even believed to help people kick morphine addiction. Doctors prescribed these types of drugs for any number of ailments. By the end of that century, though, people were beginning to understand the downsides of drug use. They were finally viewing addiction as a very real crisis, as more and more people became addicts. The US government knew that they needed to act and soon began to pass laws to regulate the drug trade. This began the criminalization of drugs in the United States. According to the National Association for the Advancement of Colored People (NAACP), between 1980 and 2015, the number of prisoners in the United States jumped from around 500,000 to 2.2 million. Of these prisoners, according

In the United States, drug use is often combated through the use of prosecution and jail sentences. But many are working to build programs using therapy to help treat addiction.

to the Bureau of Prisons, almost half (48.6 percent) have been imprisoned for drug-related crimes.

DRUG LAWS IN THE UNITED STATES

The Harrison Narcotics Act was the first national drug law implemented by the US government. Passed in 1914, the law put restrictions on marijuana, cocaine, heroin, and morphine to prevent them from being prescribed by doctors and distributed by pharmacists. Many continued to do so, however. Around five thousand physicians faced drug charges between the years 1915 and 1938 because of the Harrison Narcotics Act.

The Federal Bureau of Narcotics was formed in 1930, led by commissioner Harry Anslinger. Anslinger worked hard to not only tighten drug laws, but also to create a public aversion to drugs and drug users. To keep people from trying drugs, the Federal Bureau of Narcotics created antidrug propaganda, often portraying drug users as devil worshippers or other unsavory characters.

Drug use grew during the 1960s with increasing use of hallucinogens like LSD and psilocybin mushrooms. Many soldiers who returned from the Vietnam War came home addicted to heroin and marijuana. As a result, President Lyndon Johnson passed the Narcotics Addict Rehabilitation Act, which was one of the first laws that opened up discussion of drug addiction as a disease.

Richard Nixon was the first president to incite a massive crackdown on drug use. This is when the so-called War on Drugs

Richard Nixon, pictured here, was a staunch advocate of the War on Drugs during his administration. His work was later carried on by President Reagan.

really began. Nixon's efforts were the first that really focused on cutting off the illegal drug trade with Mexico, Colombia, and other Central and South American nations where the drugs were being produced. He created the Drug Enforcement Agency (DEA) in 1973 as a means to tackle this problem. The War on Drugs also cracked down harder on drug users themselves, calling for mandatory prison sentences for drug-related crimes.

JUST SAY NO

During the 1980s, then President Ronald Reagan took office determined to carry on the War on Drugs begun by Richard Nixon. As part of this initiative, First Lady Nancy Reagan launched the Just Say No campaign, which urged children and teens to reject drug use by simply saying no. The program quickly spread across the nation, with "Just say no" even becoming a defining catchphrase for that decade. Reagan herself made hundreds of appearances at antidrug events and even showed up on popular TV sitcoms like *Diff'rent Strokes* and *Punky Brewster* to spread the message.

Over the years, however, the campaign has faced a lot of criticism. People have complained that it oversimplified the problem of drug abuse to imply that the solution is as easy as saying no in the face of peer pressure. The program also seemed to define drug users as unsavory characters, often strangers, who were trying to lure children and teens into using drugs, when, in reality, peer pressure often comes from friends or loved ones. As Reagan said in a 1986 address to the public: "Our job is never easy because drug criminals are ingenious. They work every day to plot a new and better way to steal our children's lives, just as they've done by developing this new drug, crack. For every door that we close, they open a new door to death."

The program has been deemed ineffective. Drug Abuse Resistance Education, also known as D.A.R.E., is a program founded in 1983 that operates under the "Just say no" principle. A 2009 study at the University of Cincinnati and the University of Central Florida concluded that individuals who were enrolled in the D.A.R.E. program were just as likely to use drugs as those who weren't.

During the 1980s, children were familiar with the cartoon of McGruff the Crime Dog, whose image was used to help young people say no to drugs.

A MODERN WAR ON DRUGS

Today, the War on Drugs continues to be divisive. Many opponents of strict drug laws point to the overpopulation of prisons and the argument that these types of laws are biased, leading to a higher imprisonment rate for African Americans. According to the NAACP, African Americans are imprisoned for drug-related crimes at a rate six times higher than for white people, despite the fact that the rates of drug use among both groups are similar. Many also argue that the War on Drugs is not a war that can be won since experienced and savvy drug traffickers often simply shift how they operate rather than shut down when faced with an arrest or seizure of goods within their organization. Drug use has not gone down since 1973, when the War on Drugs began. According to DrugAbuse.gov, it's actually gone up.

Proponents of the War on Drugs insist that drug laws aren't strong enough, and that is the reason illicit substances are still such a danger to American lives. US President Donald Trump cites gang-related violence in cities, which is often tied to drugs, as a good reason to double down on drug laws. He also advocates for a more secure border with Mexico as a means to keeping drug trafficking to a minimum or cutting it off altogether.

DRUG USE AND CRIME

The laws in each state and country vary, as well as how strictly they are enforced. But the bottom line is that if you experiment with illegal drugs or use prescription drugs in a manner for which they were not intended, you are risking arrest, prosecution, and even jail time. And you don't have to be a habitual drug user to face these consequences. If you are worried about the safety of someone you know or fear that person is committing a crime, educate yourself on what actually constitutes a drug-related crime and take your concerns to someone you trust. You might discover that something that seems harmless is actually a drug offense. The following are some of the ways that people can be charged with a drug crime. Keep in mind that individuals can be charged with more than one of these crimes, which can compound the penalty exponentially.

PARAPHERNALIA

Drug paraphernalia is equipment that people use to inject, inhale, conceal, or produce an illicit substance. This includes

Possession of drug paraphernalia, even if no drugs are present during an arrest, can often lead to fines or even jail time.

syringes, pipes, or rolling papers, but also can include household items such as spoons or scales that show evidence of drug use or distribution. Even if there is no sign of illicit substances themselves, you can face charges if you are in possession of these types of items. Paraphernalia possession is most often charged as a misdemeanor but can be considered a felony in certain cases and certain states.

POSSESSION

There are two types of possession when it comes to drugs. Simple possession is when an individual has a small amount of an illicit substance for personal use. Possession with the intent to distribute alleges that an individual is in possession of a substance intended to be sold to another party. Both types of possession are considered a felony in most states and an indictable offense in Canada.

DEALING

Dealing drugs refers to selling drugs as part of a small-scale operation. This is considered a felony in all states and an indictable offense in Canada. According to the DEA, selling fewer than 50 grams (1.8 ounces) of marijuana can lead to five years in prison and a $250,000 fine. Larger amounts can be considered trafficking, which carries with it a much more severe sentence.

TRAFFICKING

Trafficking constitutes the import, sale, and transport of a large amount of a controlled substance. If authorities simply believe that your intent was to do any of these things, you can be charged with trafficking. This is a felony that carries a sentence from between three years and life in prison.

MANUFACTURING AND GROWING

Growing or manufacturing illicit drugs can include being involved in any step of the process, including providing equipment or chemicals (as in the production of methamphetamine). Even if you are not the one in charge of the operation, the smallest involvement is punishable by law. Drug manufacturing is a felony.

CHAPTER 5

THE ROAD TO RECOVERY FROM STIMULANT ABUSE

Now that you understand stimulant addiction and the effects that these types of drugs have on the body and on your life, what comes next? You might find this to be one of the hardest questions you've ever had to answer, especially if you are dealing with your own drug addiction. Recovery from addiction is undoubtedly the healthiest path to take, but it can also be scary and challenging and might sometimes result in a relapse. This is why you should fully understand why recovery is important, how to give yourself (or the addict in your life) the tools to recover successfully, and know ways to give and receive ongoing support that will keep addiction at bay in the future.

REASONS FOR RECOVERY

Whether you or someone you love is living with drug addiction, it's important to know why recovery is the right path. Let's take a look at some good reasons to quit.

On the road to recovery, loved ones are often an important component of your support network. Recovery is a process of healing for people who love the addict as well.

PHYSICAL HEALTH

Methamphetamine and other stimulants are hard on the entire body, but especially the brain and nervous system. Meth users often experience memory loss and a shorter attention span. But a 2005 study published in an issue of the *Archives of General Psychiatry* showed that the brain does work to repair itself. After a year of avoiding the substance, damage to the brain can be partially or even completely reversed. Long-term use of prescription amphetamines can actually lead to chronic fatigue. Quitting these types of drugs allows the body to eventually function normally again, allowing the user to feel physically healthier.

Drug treatment is often very expensive, but some programs can work within a budget. Speak to a doctor, therapist, or drug counselor to help find the right program for you.

FINANCIAL WELL-BEING

Drug use is expensive, and drug abuse can lead to financial distress, even homelessness. Back on a healthier path, former addicts can work toward independence and financial stability again. They can explore things that were possibly out of reach in the past because of financial instability, like traveling and taking up hobbies.

FRIENDS AND FAMILY

The stress that drug use can have on family and friends can be permanently damaging to personal relationships. Leaving drugs behind can help rebuild those relationships and allow a person to participate in other people's lives once again. Friends and family can also play a crucial role in recovery by offering support, which can help an addict avoid a relapse.

HAVING A FUTURE

Perhaps the most important reason to pursue recovery from drug addiction is to build a future for yourself. In 2015, 52,404 people died of a drug overdose. The reality is that stimulant abuse can be deadly.

TYPES OF REHABILITATION PROGRAMS AND TREATMENTS

Finding the right rehabilitation program for you can be challenging and expensive, so it's important to explore your options and make the best decision for you. Your choice will depend on the severity of the addiction, the type of drug and symptoms of withdrawal, and your physical and financial ability to pursue treatment. Let's take a look at some of the most common treatment options.

RESIDENTIAL TREATMENT

Long- and short-term residential treatment facilities are places where patients live for a period of time—between three weeks and a year—in order to detox safely and then examine their addictive behaviors within a group environment where drugs are virtually unavailable. Some residential treatment programs work with clients to help them reintegrate into society through job counseling and other support services.

THE EXPENSE OF DRUG TREATMENT

Drug treatment can be expensive, but the good news is that financial aid or financing is often available, and some insurance plans cover addiction care. Be sure to weigh financial factors in order to make an informed decision about the right treatment for you.

- Detox and outpatient rehabilitation can cost between $1,000 and $1,500 just for detox. Rehabilitation and long-term care can make this option more expensive, topping out at around $10,000 for a well-known rehab center, such as the Betty Ford clinic.
- Shorter inpatient programs can range from $6,000 to $20,000, depending on the amenities available and the length of stay. Longer programs, ranging from sixty to ninety days, can cost between $12,000 and $60,000.
- Medication intended to help with detox and recovery can be an expense all on its own, although this kind of medication is usually limited to alcohol and opiate addiction. Methadone treatment costs around $4,700 per year.
- Individual therapy programs are often covered by insurance or may be available on a sliding scale payment plan. Student therapy programs are often available at low cost.
- Group therapy and support can often be found free of charge through groups like AA and Narcotics Anonymous. Look for programs in your area by searching online or through a medical professional.

The benefits of this type of treatment are that the intensive nature of the program makes it virtually impossible to get access to drugs and builds a support base around the recovering addict. Some negative aspects are that this type of program can be expensive and addicts must spend time away from friends and family during treatment.

OUTPATIENT TREATMENT

Outpatient treatment programs offer the same type of therapy and recovery services as residential programs but allow clients to continue living at home. Some offer day programs in which a patient comes back for regularly scheduled intensive treatments. This type of treatment is often recommended for individuals with a strong social support network. The benefits of this type of program are that patients can continue to live their lives on their own schedules, they're often more affordable than residential programs, and patients have access to friends and family. Many treatment facilities also take insurance.

INDIVIDUALIZED DRUG COUNSELING

The right option for you might be meeting personally with a therapist who is trained in drug counseling. This type of therapist can help you get to the bottom of your drug addiction and help form some long-term coping strategies. The benefits of this type of treatment are that drug counselors provide long-term support and usually take insurance (or payments on a sliding scale). The downside is that they cannot help you through the physical symptoms of detox, so drug counseling must be combined with another type of treatment during the early stages of recovery.

Group counseling can be a beneficial and low-cost option. Talk to a doctor, therapist, or drug counselor to help find the right group for you.

GROUP COUNSELING

Group counseling can be beneficial in many ways. It's often a low-cost option, and recovering addicts can spend time around other recovering addicts, giving and receiving support as needed. As with individual drug counseling, there is no detox support available through group counseling, so, if possible, speak to a doctor about your options for dealing with the symptoms of withdrawal.

SELF-CARE DURING RECOVERY

Whether you are an addict or your loved one is, it's important to remember to take care of yourself during recovery, both mentally and physically. Self-care can describe just relaxing with a good book some night, making an emergency therapy session when you need one, or calling your sponsor to make sure you have support. Self-care can include exercise and healthy eating. It can include making plans for the future and setting goals. It can include just telling yourself that it's going to be okay every night before you go to bed. Little things can go a long way toward helping you along the road to recovery.

TEN GREAT QUESTIONS
TO ASK ASK A DRUG COUNSELOR

1. What is your personal approach to drug treatment?

2. How do I explain to friends and family what's going on with me?

3. Where can I go for help if I feel like I might relapse?

4. What happens if I relapse?

5. What can I expect from recovery?

6. What if I can't afford drug treatment in the long term?

7. How effective will this treatment be?

8. What can I do to curb future behaviors that might lead me back to addiction?

9. Should I worry about becoming addicted to any medications that the doctor prescribes to help curb drug abuse?

10. What type of treatment is right for me?

GLOSSARY

ADHD Attention deficit hyperactivity disorder is a brain disorder characterized by a shorter attention span and sometimes hyperactivity.

AMPHETAMINE A type of stimulant often used to treat certain brain disorders but that can lead to abuse as well.

BIPOLAR DISORDER A disorder characterized by periods of heightened activity, followed by periods of depression.

CAFFEINE A stimulant found in certain plants (coffee, tea, and cacao beans) that can have the effect of heightening energy.

DETOX The first step in any recovery program, during which the addict withdraws from the drug.

DOPAMINE A neurotransmitter in the brain that is released during moments of happiness, creating the happy feeling in the brain.

FELONY The most serious type of crime, often resulting in prison time.

MDMA Sometimes called ecstasy, MDMA is a drug that can temporararily alter mood and awareness when ingested.

METHAMPHETAMINE A powerful stimulant, often distributed in the form of crystals, which can be highly addictive.

MISDEMEANOR A crime that is more serious than an infraction but less serious than a felony. These types of crimes can result in a fine or jail time.

NARCOLEPSY A sleep disorder that results in excessive sleepiness, often leading to involuntary sleep episodes.

NEUROTRANSMITTERS Chemical messengers released in the brain that bond with neuron receptors, resulting in an emotional impact.

NICOTINE A chemical found in tobacco (and in small traces in some other plants) that acts as a stimulant when consumed.

OVERDOSE The ingestion of a drug in a larger amount than the body can process, resulting in seizure, unconsciousness, or even death.

PARAPHERNALIA Items used for making, consuming, or concealing drugs.

PTSD Post-traumatic stress disorder; a trauma-based disorder that can often result in a flight-or-flight reaction in situations that are not dangerous.

REHABILITATION The process of restoring good health, beginning with detox and continuing with long-term coping strategies and therapy.

REWARD CIRCUIT The parts of the brain responsible for releasing dopamine.

STIMULANT A type of drug characterized by heightened energy and elation.

TOXICOLOGY A branch of science wherein the safety and effects of drugs on the body are studied.

WITHDRAWAL The body's natural reaction to no longer being exposed to a drug upon which it has become dependent. Symptoms can include mental distress, insomnia, and depression; physical effects can include sweating, nausea, and tremors. Extreme cases of withdrawal can result in seizure, stroke, or heart attack.

FOR MORE INFORMATION

Addiction Center
Recovery Worldwide LLC
121 South Orange Avenue, Suite 1450
Orlando, FL 32801
(877) 416-1550
Website: https://www.addictioncenter.com
Facebook: @TheAddictionCenter
Twitter: @AddictionCentr
Addiction Center is an online guide to help those struggling with
addiction find help locally.

Canadian Centre on Substance Use and Addiction
500-75 Albert Street
Ottawa, ON K1P 5E7
Canada
(613) 235-4048
Website: http://www.ccsa.ca
Twitter: @CCSACanada
CCSA works to address issues related to substance abuse and
addiction across Canada.

Twitter: @DrugFreeAmerica

Drug Free America Foundation is a drug prevention program that helps to develop policies that block illegal drug use and addiction.

Drug Free Kids Canada (DFK Canada)

PO Box 23103

Toronto, ON M5N 3A8

Canada

(416) 479-6972

Website: https://www.drugfreekidscanada.org

Facebook: @DrugFreeKidsCanada

Twitter: @DrugFreeKidsCda

Drug Free Kids Canada offers guidance to parents of teens dealing with drug abuse issues and works with agencies to produce antidrug content.

Hazelden Betty Ford Foundation

PO Box 11

Center City, MN 55012-0011

(866) 296-7404

Website: http://www.hazeldenbettyford.org

Facebook: @hazeldenbettyfordfoundation

Twitter: @hazldnbettyford

The Hazelden Betty Ford Foundation is the largest nonprofit drug and alcohol addiction treatment center in the United States.

National Institute on Drug Abuse (NIDA)

Office of Science Policy and Communications

Public Information and Liaison Branch

6001 Executive Boulevard

Room 5213, MSC 9561

Bethesda, MD 20892

(301) 443-1124

Website: https://www.drugabuse.gov

Facebook: @NIDANIH

Twitter: @NIDAnews

NIDA is a scientific research institute, operating under the US Department of Health and Human Services, which works to research drug abuse and addiction, prevention, and drug treatment.

FOR FURTHER READING

Ambrose, Marylou, and Veronica Deisler. *Investigate Methamphetamine*. New York, NY: Enslow, 2015.

Barnes, Henrietta Robin. *Hijacked Brains: The Experience and Science of Chronic Addiction*. Hanover, NH: Dartmouth, 2015.

Barnett, Robin. *Addict in the House: A No-Nonsense Family Guide Through Addiction and Recovery*. Oakland, CA: New Harbinger, 2016.

Beattie, Melody. *Codependent No More: How to Stop Controlling Others and Start Caring for Yourself*. Center City, MN: Hazelden, 1986.

Bowser, Benjamin P., Carl O. Word, and Toby Seddon. *Understanding Drug Use and Abuse: A Global Perspective*. New York, NY: Palgrave, 2014.

Eldridge, Alison, and Stephen Eldridge. *Investigate Club Drugs*. New York, NY: Enslow, 2015.

Foxman, Paul. *The Clinician's Guide to Anxiety Disorders in Kids & Teens*. Eau Claire, WI: PESI Publishing, 2016.

Hari, Johann. *Chasing the Scream: The First and Last Days of the War on Drugs*. New York, NY: Bloomsbury USA, 2016.

Perritano, John. Stimulants: *Meth, Cocaine, and Amphetamines*. Broomall, PA: Mason Crest, 2017.

Waters, Rosa. *Methamphetamine & Other Amphetamines* (Downside of Drugs). Broomall, PA: Mason Crest, 2014.

BIBLIOGRAPHY

ABC News. "Meth Makes Winter Deadly for Young Couple." March 3, 2005. http://abcnews.go.com/Health/Primetime /story?id=549455&page=1.

AddictionCenter. "Cost of Drug and Alcohol Rehab." Retrieved September 12, 2017. https://www.addictioncenter.com /rehab-questions/cost-of-drug-and-alcohol-treatment.

Associated Press. "Brain May Repair Itself When Meth Users Quit." *Fox News*, April 6, 2005. http://www.foxnews.com /story/2005/04/06/brain-may-repair-itself-when-meth-users -quit.amp.html.

Bonn, Scott A. "Prescription Drugs Are More Deadly Than Street Drugs." *Psychology Today*, April 28, 2014. https://www .psychologytoday.com/blog/wicked-deeds/201404 /prescription-drugs-are-more-deadly-street-drugs.

Brookshire, Bethany. "Dopamine Is _____." *Slate*, July 3, 2013. http://www.slate.com/articles/health_and_science /science/2013/07/what_is_dopamine_love_lust_sex _addiction_gambling_motivation_reward.html.

Carey, Benedict. "Carrie Fisher Put Pen and Voice in Service of 'Bipolar Pride.'" *NY Times*, December 28, 2017. https://www .nytimes.com/2016/12/28/health/carrie-fisher-bipolar -disorder.html.

FindLaw. "Types of Drug Crimes." Retrieved September 10, 2017. http://criminal.findlaw.com/criminal-charges/types-of -drug-crimes.html.

Foundation for a Drug-Free World. "History of Methamphetamine." Retrieved August 31, 2017. http://www.drugfreeworld.org /drugfacts/crystalmeth/history-of-methamphetamine.html.

Fowler, Gretchen. "Toxicologist Says Meth Impaired Couple Who Died in Storm." *Grand Island Independent*, January 22, 2005. http://www.theindependent.com/news/toxicologist-says -meth-impaired-couple-who-died-in-storm /article_45c21aab-ac5e-5736-95f1-ec23e9b111a2.html.

Guarnotta, Emily. "Meth Overdose." DrugAbuse.com. Retrieved August 31, 2017. http://drugabuse.com/library /meth-overdose.

Kelly, Michael B. "World Drug Report Reveals the Staggering Extent of North America's Meth Problem." *Business Insider*, June 26, 2013. http://www.businessinsider.com /north-america-has-a-massive-meth-problem-2013-6.

Lilienfeld, Scott O. and Hal Arkowitz. "Why 'Just Say No' Doesn't Work." *Scientific American*, January 1, 2014. https://www .scientificamerican.com/article/why-just-say-no-doesnt -work.

Lombardi, Lisa. "Is Drug Addiction Genetic?" *ABC News*, September 25, 2014. http://abcnews.go.com/Health /Wellness/drug-addiction-genetic/story?id=25728024#3.

NAACP. "Criminal Justice Fact Sheet." Retrieved September 5, 2017. http://www.naacp.org/criminal-justice-fact-sheet.

National Institute of Drug Abuse. "Types of Treatment Programs." Retrieved September 7, 2017. https://www.drugabuse.gov /publications/principles-drug-addiction-treatment-research -based-guide-third-edition/drug-addiction-treatment-in -united-states/types-treatment-programs.

National Institute of Drug Abuse. "What Is Methamphetamine?" Retrieved August 31, 2017. https://www.drugabuse.gov /publications/drugfacts/methamphetamine.

National Institute of Mental Health. "Brain Basics." Retrieved August 27, 2017. https://www.nimh.nih.gov/health /educational-resources/brain-basics/brain-basics.shtml.

Recovery Village, The. "The Dangers of Methamphetamine: Ingredients and How It's Made." Retrieved August 27, 2017. https://www.therecoveryvillage.com/meth-addiction /dangers-methamphetamine-ingredients-made/#gref.

Shen, Aviva. "The Disastrous Legacy of Nancy Reagan's 'Just Say No' Campaign." ThinkProgress, March 6, 2016. https:// thinkprogress.org/the-disastrous-legacy-of-nancy-reagans -just-say-no-campaign-fd24570bf109.

Tribune news services. "More Than 50,000 Overdose Deaths: A Grim Tally Soars to All-Time U.S. High." *Chicago Tribune*, December 8, 2016. http://www.chicagotribune.com/news /nationworld/ct-us-overdose-deaths-20161208-story.html.

INDEX

ABOUT THE AUTHOR

Bethany Bryan is the author of multiple books for Rosen Publishing and an editor of comics and nonfiction. She decided to study the topic of methamphetamine use after hearing the story of the deaths of Janelle Hornickel and Michael Wamsley. She is a strong advocate for therapy and self-care and urges people to seek the help they need.

PHOTO CREDITS

Cover Photographee.eu/Shutterstock.com; p. 5 David Handschuh/ NY Daily News Archive/Getty Images; pp. 7, 17, 26, 35, 44 (top) Kaesler Media/Shutterstock.com; p. 7 Science & Society Picture Library/Getty Images; p. 8 edwardolive/iStock/Thinkstock; p. 12 David Pollack/Corbis Historical/Getty Images; p. 13 Daniel Roland /AFP/Getty Images; p. 18 BISP/Universal Images Group /Getty Images; p. 20 JGI/Jamie Grill/Getty Images; p. 23 Mike Watson Images/moodboard/Thinkstock; p. 24 Joe Raedle /Getty Images; p. 27 Andrew Aitchison/Corbis Historical /Getty Images; p. 29 AlexRaths/iStock/Thinkstock; p. 31 Paul Archuleta/FilmMagic/Getty Images; p. 32 Axelie/Bauer-Griffin /FilmMagic/Getty Images; p. 36 Darrin Kilmek/DigitalVision /Thinkstock; p. 37 Don Carl Steffen/Gamma-Rapho/Getty Images; p. 39 Smith Collection/Gado/Archive Photos/Getty Images; p. 41 Pacific Press/LightRocket/Getty Images; p. 45 Voisin/Phanie /Canopy/Getty Images; p. 46 moodboard/Thinkstock; p. 50 KatarzynaBialasiewicz/iStock/Thinkstock.

Design and Layout: Nicole Russo-Duca; Editor and Photo Researcher: Elizabeth Schmermund